Words

PURPOSE

LOVE

CHANGE

FAITH

live

DREAM

HOPE

reflection

beauty

vision

To Inspire
VOLUME 1

Paul A. Blake

Acknowledgement

The following persons have worked tirelessly to make this book a reality and are deserving of thanks Francis Yorke and Matthew Blake and who edited draft after draft. Andrew Blake for design and graphics work to done to perfection. Thanks to the countless other persons in my life both friends and family who have inspired me in ways that I cannot possibly explain. To the "Class of 91" Manchester High School I express thanks to you all, years may have pass but together we all continue to reach for the stars, the greatest inspiration we have is the bond of friendship. To the countless brothers and sister of the Church of Christ family I say thanks your love and confidence have kept me going even when I was un-sure of my own abilities. Last but by no means least thanks to Almighty God who made all this possible and to all my family. Many thanks to all and God bless.

Copyright

Table of Contents

Table of Contents

Words to Inspire: Volume One

Experiencing the power of words

Introduction

Why bother to dream?

It is said "there are many dreams lying in the graveyard". Why should we not just settle for any stations in life and accept the fact that the majority of people in this world will never be able to realize their hearts desire. Why should we even dare to dream about becoming more than what we are now? If all of life is going to eventually end with us dying why should we bother pursuing anything else than just the basics of food, clothes and shelter? Why bother to dream?

This great world was built on dreams. Dreams are responsible for the birth of nations; dreams have broken the chains of poverty and destitution; dreams have restored pride and hope in people who would have been otherwise tossed on garbage dump of society; dreams have allowed the weak to find strength; dreams have moved individuals to claim justice in an otherwise unjust world; dreams are responsible for the survival of nations, families, and friendships. Dreams have always touched our lives in every way that can be imagined.

What if we could not dream? What if there was nothing to look forward to other that what we know now? It is alright to dream; no one has ever achieved anything in this world without first dreaming about it. Dream big because this world is your playground and there is no limit to what you can accomplish in this life.

Would this world know the name of Marcus Mosiah Garvey if he did not dream he had a purpose? Would America have a black president if Martin Luther King Jr., did not have a dream of equality and justice for all humanity regardless of class, colour or creed?? Would Usain Bolt and Shelly-Ann Fraser-Pryce be the world's fastest man and woman if they did not dream about standing on the podium of victory? Could our ancestors chart the way for our freedom without first dreaming of it?

Where would any one of us be today without having first dreamt about where we are? Dreams are the doors which open to a world of possibilities.

To the young man who sees only suffering as the path to his future, I say start dreaming of who and what you can become. To the young woman who has been told that she is no good, I say dream your way to the mountain top. To that child who is told that they are good for nothing, plant the seed of a positive dream and grow to reap everything. It is your right to dream, allow no one to rob you of this awesome phenomenon. It is with just one dream that this world can be changed in a single moment.

Dream because you have an imagination that has no limits, let no one control the boundaries of your thoughts. Dream because you are alive and full of hope, no matter how down you are today dreams will lift you up on the wings of tomorrow. Dream because you refuse to give in to the small-mindedness of doubters who never see the cloud with the silver lining. Dream because you do not need the approval of anyone to explore your heights of endless possibilities.

Don't just dream small dreams but dream big dreams because you are larger than life. Don't settle for dreams of insignificant things but dreams that will leave your footprints on the face of this earth. Don't dream about yesterday when tomorrow stands as an unchartered course waiting to be discovered. Don't dream of finding love but rather dream that you are what define love. Don't dream of what you can be, rather dream that you are exactly who you want to be.

Why bother to dream? You will never know what this great world holds for you unless you dare to dream. You will never know the awesome power that lies within you unless you dream. You never know how much your actions can affect this world unless you dream. Dreams are not meant to take us away from reality; they are there to remind us that we are all creatures destined for greatness as part of God's grand design.

1

Don't allow your future to be charted by past failures.

The curse of failure will follow many people to their graves. They fail to go after their dreams because they are constantly plagued by one or multiple failures. If you should look at the people in the past who failed but did not allow their failure to determine their future success you would find that you are not alone. Albert Einstein was treated as a dunce because he had a learning disability; Thomas Edison failed at his light bulb invention over a hundred times before he got it right; Marcus Garvey failed at several business ventures but refused to give up. Failure is a part of life; it is what paves the way to success.

As you journey through life you will not fail only once, but many times before you taste sweet success. Don't allow the failure you experience to be that which charts your future. Each time you experience failure in your life it is one more opportunity to learn some great lesson. It is one more opportunity to learn what you need to do to be successful the next time you try.

Successful people don't walk around carrying a sign of failure with them. They evaluate why they failed and do all in their power to avoid the pitfalls of failure the next time around. If you allow failure to follow you around, you will never be able to reach the goal of successful living. Today is the day you must decide to throw off the chains of failure and say to yourself I AM BUILT FOR SUCCESS!

2

The greatest tragedy in life is to have lived without a purpose

Floating through life is definitely not the ideal option for the majority of persons. Most of the time there is an innate desire to reach for something more. The truth is, we often don't discover our true purpose and so lose out on experiencing joy and happiness in our lives. Don't settle for going through life always asking what is my purpose? Instead make a deliberate effort to find your place in this world and leave behind a meaningful contribution.

Find your purpose, step out in faith and challenge yourself to be much more than you are now. Never be contented to sit idly and watch others change the world. People who have changed the course of history did not do so because they were born great. They accomplished the impossible because they were courageous and would not take no for an answer. They realized that they were here for a reason and they committed them-selves to finding what that reason was. Marcus Garvey will never know the legacy that he has left behind, this was because of his refusal to allow others to dictate his place in this great universe.

It is not what you get out of life that you will be remembered for, it is what you contributed to living. Live for someone or something besides yourself. Your purpose is that one thing that constantly fills your soul, that thing you just can't seem to let go until it has been done. It is that dream that will make an impact in the life of someone somewhere in the world and if you don't do it the world would have lost out on a wonderful opportunity to witness something great.!

3

Change is inevitable, don't fear it; embrace it.

I cannot help but remember the book "Who Moved My Cheese?" by Spencer Johnson when reflecting on the above quote. So many people are not prepared for change though it is the one thing that always remains constant in our lives. Just as often as we breathe the air around us so is the inevitability of change. No matter what you do or how much you try to avoid it change is a factor of life. If you are not prepared to change, you are only setting yourself up for a lifetime of disappointments and frustrations. The cheese is always going to be on the move.

Why fear something that you cannot control? Our response to the change when it does happen, is the only activity we can control. Your fear of change will cause you to miss out on opportunities, behaving like the ostrich with its head buried in the sand. If you fear change you're resigning to a life without excitement or possibility, because you are fearful you will never be willingly to go beyond your comfort zone. Yes, change may bring uncertainty but change also opens the doors of adventure and opportunity. Even with your many fears the cheese will still move.

Embrace change even if you are not sure of what is on the other side of the door. Accepting change is taking the chance to learn something new. Why settle for being in the same place all the time when the world is your playground. Be willing to go on the other side of the maze to see if there is more cheese waiting for you. Until you decide to go with change you find yourself stuck in the past while change is happening in real time. Every aspect of life from birth through to death brings change; if you accept or reject change it will still happen; if you bury your head in the sand or fear change it will still happen. The only way to really handle change when it comes your way is to say here I am, I am ready. Each time the cheese moves move with it.

4

Life's challenges are simply mind over matter, if you don't mind they don't matter.

There will always be challenges in our lives. It is what we think about these challenges that makes the difference in how we handle them. If we see our challenges as mountains that are impossible to get over, we will treat them as such. Rather than trying to find our way around the mountain we allow it to fall on us, simply because we see it as a source of defeat rather than a possible victory. Imagine if we could learn to view life's challenges as just one more hurdle we need to get over and no matter what we are going to find a way to get over it.

How we respond to challenges will either make or break us. We can choose to make them complications or decide to accept them as character builders. We can allow that challenge to be a mountain blocking our vision or we can decide go around it to see what's on the other side. Each time we come upon a difficulty in our lives we stand at the crossroads of where positive and negative responses meet. The direction we decide to take will be strongly impacted by how we view the difficulty before us. Challenges will be challenges, they don't change. The only change that occurs is the change we decide to make. If we decide to not make our challenges overwhelm us, we will move quicker to finding solutions. They may have us down for a little while, but because we are focused of finding solutions we will never find comfort in defeat. When we tell ourselves that we are winners, we begin to think like winners and our challenges become stories of success. Challenges are simply mind over matter, if we don't mind they don't matter.

5

Though I may be broken you will not see me fall to pieces.

Sometimes life is about fighting. There are battles that you will win, others you will lose but the key is to keep on fighting. None of us know which of life's circumstances will get us down. Even the best of us tend to fall apart at one time or another but falling apart does not mean defeat. When life gets us down in the dumps it is a good place to begin to strategize. It is while down in the dumps many times the opportunity for self-examination becomes useful. All the mistakes made and opportunities missed must be viewed from a new perspective. This is not the time to give up and feel sorry that nothing you tried is going right. But it is an opportunity to see if some important signs were ignored along the way.

Brokenness is often paired with success. Almost every successful person has had to stand at the intersection of defeat and decisions. The direction taken will depend on how the current state or circumstance is understood. One can decide to just simply give in and fall apart or choose to pick up the pieces and mend them into opportunities leading to success. If you ever find yourself broken it simply means that it is time for to begin seeking out the glue of opportunity that holds things together.

6

You reap what you sow why not commit to sowing seed of success.

Every decision we make will either add to or take away from our success. The principle of reaping what you sow does not only apply to how we should treat each other but can also be applicable on a personal level. If we sow the correct seeds in our lives, then we will surely reap the fruits of our labour. The seeds referred are the opportunities that we can choose to or refuse to make use of each day. We may never know how making use of an opportunity today, will turn out for us tomorrow.

Success does not occur over night. Imagine that every farmer already knows the outcome of the seeds they plant. As long as the elements are right, the fruits of their labour will be realized. Yet farmers sit in anticipation month after month waiting to seeds blossom into flowers and flowers grow into healthy fruit. They do this each year without failure, they never fail to plant their seeds. The end result is success, but the seeds must first be planted. If we are going to be successful we have to begin to plant seeds of opportunity today. It may be helping someone to do something you really don't like doing. It may mean volunteering for a project in your community; it can be giving some of your time at church or school. We may not see how these can turn out to be opportunities for success but that's just how life works, opportunities for success visit in the most unlikely places.

If you know where you are coming from, you will know where you are going, if you know where you are going, you will get there through perseverance and hard work.

So many people in this world would be better off if they only knew their place in this life. We often don't fulfill our purpose because we understand so very little of how our past affects us. This is not to say that we should drown ourselves in the sorrows of the past but any understanding of our present circumstances and future opportunities begins with knowing how where we are coming from, and this affects even the choices we are making now. We cannot change the past but we can use our knowledge of it to inform how we make decisions today and prepare ourselves to grasp future opportunities.

One of the things that keep many people from moving forward is looking back at past mistakes and failures. We keep looking back at past failures and mistakes not wanting to repeat them and somehow convince ourselves that this is for our own good. The only good thing about looking back at the past is that it arms us with information we need to do to move forward.

Let the past remain where it should be, behind you. When you have discovered your purpose begin to move towards it with enthusiasm. Now that you know how where you are coming from has helped to shape who you are, don't dwell too long in the land of looking back. Have a clear vision of future success and put things in place to help you achieve your goals. The past and present have provided enough signs that can help to enhance your outlook on life. Now you have a clear vision of what lies ahead move forward with perseverance and hard work.

8

Your destiny is not written in the stars but in your desire for excellence.

Some people are satisfied living their lives based on luck. They are always waiting for the best to happen to them while doing very little to make anything actually happen. You are not here by mere circumstances but you are here by purpose and design. Our ability to succeed rest upon understanding of these two things. To be lucky is not a rule of life but merely an exception, the vast majority of successful people in this world had to work extremely hard and you and I are no different.

Success begins with dreams; dreams turn into desire and desire seeks out opportunity. If you are spending more time hoping to get lucky than actually working towards success you will find yourself constantly disappointed. Just think of the time wasted waiting to have luck change your circumstances. All of that time could better spent seeking out opportunities that will bring the success you so crave. The majority of people in this world who have had to wait for luck to change their circumstances have found themselves facing bitter disappointment. Luck is really an exception, not a rule.

Success is not found in horoscopes, Ouija boards, tarot cards and such things. It begins with a having a passion for achieving something greater and committing to pursuing it even if it requires blood, sweat and tears. Every decision that you make today will pave the way towards your destiny. We write our own stories, luck and chance are simply ingredients that may be picked up along the way, but are insignificant to the final outcome of the novel of success. If you desire to be successful take charge of your own destiny and begin to write your story.

9

There is no shame in failure, only shame in accepting defeat.

Show me someone who has never failed at anything and I will tell you that person has never tried anything. Failure is one of those things that walk hand in hand with success. We will all fail at something. Even after you have laid the best plans to be successful you will experience failure in one form or another. So when it comes down to the wire there is no shame in failure as a matter of fact there is much be learned from failure.

Expect to fail but refuse to accept defeat. Each time you fail at doing anything it is an opportunity to get it right next time. Giving in to feelings of defeat to the point where they cripple your next effort is to give up the satisfaction of knowing the unknown. Accepting defeat is drowning yourself in a pool of self-pity refusing to see that you are powerful beyond measure. Life will knock you down every now and then but the choice of staying down or getting up is always in your hands.

Refuse to accept defeat even if the evidence before you say otherwise because there is that single spark of opportunity that will always present itself. If you throw up your hands in defeat you may miss out on the chance the step into greatness. Every time life throws you a knockout blow shake it off and step into the ring for one more round. The next time may be the difference between hanging your head in shame or walking proud, because even though you are defeated now, you will be back again. Refuse to accept defeat!

10

When you have found your purpose pursue it as if it were your last day on earth.

You have only one life to live so don't waste precious time chasing after insignificant things. Finding your purpose is of utmost importance to your success. When you have found your purpose embrace and pursue as if your life depends on it. It is not enough to simply dream about what you want to do with your time on earth, you should strive to leave your footprints etched in the sands of time. Approach life with an urgency that there are many things you need to get done and have very little time to do them. What if you knew today was your last day on earth? How would you spend it? And what would you do? So many people are plagued by these questions because they are yet to find their purpose. They simply float through life never planting any roots or laying a foundation to be successful. These are persons who will forever be experiencing the elusive dream of always having a desire for something greater but never achieving it because they are without purpose. Challenge yourself to find and fulfill your purpose pursue it with all you have inside.

Pursue your purpose as if you have nothing to lose, as if this is your one chance to shine. Never allow yourself to settle for an existence of just being ordinary when you were created to be extra-ordinary. Great men and women were never born naturally great; it was not in their gene pool. What they did was discover their purpose and pursued it as if their lives depended on it. Everything that you are now and all that you will ever be is dependent on you finding your true worth and purpose. Do you know your purpose?

11

Life will sometimes lead you on the most unlikely paths so make plans for the opportunities you find there.

Many people will miss out on perfect opportunities because of failure to realize when an opportunity is presenting itself. The path to successful living is where preparation meets opportunity, therefore our responsibility is to make sure we are walking on the correct path. Though opportunity is found on the most unlikely of paths, not all paths look the same. Life does not tell us where it is going to lead us, but it does prepare us well by paving the way with opportunities.

There is a common saying "expect the unexpected" that often plays itself out in our lives one way or another. We don't always know where life will lead us and we are often caught off guard because it is rather difficult to make plans for unexpected opportunities. Life is a journey and sometimes it takes us down pathways that we have not planned for but the opportunities found there may be life changing. Expecting the unexpected means to be aware we may not control where life leads us but we can surely make good use of the journey along the way.

Be prepared for the unexpected opportunities. It's not a matter of if they will come but simply a matter of when. When they do come embrace them as a part of the journey on the road to success. Don't design your life in such a way that there is no room for the unexpected. Don't place so many roadblocks on your pathway that unexpected opportunities cannot get around them. Every road that life leads us down is so designed to give us a push into the future, even those that have unexpected opportunities.

12

How many lessons have you learned from your failures?

If you never learn anything from your failures, it is likely that you will keep on failing. Not many people will be able to tell the story of getting it right the first time, you have to brace yourself for failure. The problem is not really how many times you fail but that so often no significant lesson is taken from failure. The lessons learned from failure can be a gateway for future success. Each time you fail at any task it is one more rung up the ladder of success.

The value of lessons learned is dependent on how failure is viewed. Do you see your failure as a reason for giving up or a reason to keep on trying? Those who view failure as an excuse for giving up will never look for lessons and will keep trying new things only to fail again. Those who see failure as an opportunity to learn will spend time working out the details that caused failure in the first place, so as not to fail again at the same task. If no lessons are forthcoming from failing then the result will a constant going around in circles, always coming back to the same place, asking the same question why I am here again?

Learn from your failures. Don't go back to making the same mistakes again and again. Your failures are just reminders of what you must avoid doing the next time around. Each time you fail write it down, analyze and then make a new plan, because you now have more useful information to move forward. Life's lessons are only useful if they teach us what we need to know. So there is no harm done in failing, the harm comes when you learn nothing and making the same mistakes becomes what defines you. What lessons have you learnt from your failures?

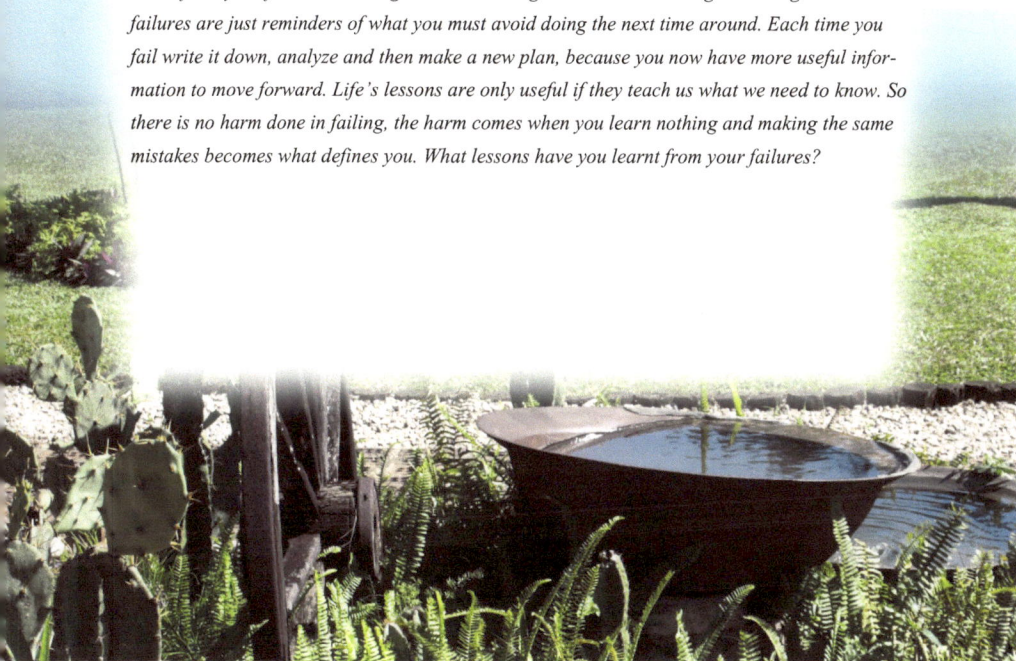

13

You are here, by no one's desire and design but God's.

How often do you find yourself asking the question why am I here? Am I here by chance or because of the intentional design of one greater than myself? You are not an accident you were deliberately planted on this earth with a specific purpose in mind. The blueprint for your life has already been drawn up by God and all that you need to know is what are the dimensions that you need to fulfill. Because you are here by God's desire and design there is no need to live your life shaped by the whims and fancies of people who have no good outcome for your life. God has already declared you to be a success story.

When you find yourself asking why you are here just, contemplate asking why should you not be? Why should you not be a part of this great universe? You are here because the great God of heaven saw something in you that this the world requires. You did not just happen to be born in this geographical location, in this moment of history, but because without you in it, the world as we know it would be so much different. Among all of God's creatures there is none like you and as long as humanity survives there will never be another. This alone should strengthen your resolve that you are a product desired and designed by God.

No one has the power to alter the course of your life but God. Even in the midst of the most tragic circumstances he can still complete his blueprint for your life. Don't allow what others think your life should be to be that which causes you to lose focus on what God has planned out for you. He designed you with purpose and the ability to fit perfectly into the space that he has carved out just for you. When he steps back and views the person he created, it satisfies him so much that he will say "it is good to have fashioned such a one full of purpose and potential".

14

Live one day at a time looking forward to the days ahead.

In all the hustle and bustle of life, learning to live life one day at a time is a true treasure. Too many times people lose sight of what is really meaningful because they spent so much time focusing and worrying about what is ahead, that the present becomes a blur. Living life one day at a time means learning how to accept today for what it is and doing the best to make sure that all the opportunities that it has to offer have been put to good use. It means being appreciative of the simple moments that come with being alive at the present time and not being overly concerned about the possibility of not being able to see tomorrow.

Some may view this as a very careless way to live one's life, but it begs this question even if the best plans are made for tomorrow what guarantee is there that it will work out that way? This is not to suggest that it is all right to wander through life aimlessly and without purpose but it is an encouragement not to wrest with life's uncertain things when the present is always waiting in the wings. So many people wake up each day planning for life tomorrow; to be more loving, more successful; more outgoing; more attentive; without ever actually realizing any of these things. The key to living one day at a time is to make a concerted effort to strive to achieve new things each day without missing a beat.

Life is too short to live life always thinking ahead. Learn how to live each day in the present. When life is lived in the present it presents a clearer picture of what lies ahead. Living one day at a time is to achieve the best out of every day. It is waking up each day and taking time out to smell the flowers despite the volume of work you have. It is making a deliberate effort to let someone know how special they are to you and being genuine about it. It is accepting your limitations knowing you will never be able to accomplish all you set out to do because you are only human. It is taking those fifteen minute breaks in your day or that one hour of lunch to just engage someone in healthy conversation about a subject that you consider important enough to discuss. It is just going outside for a while and standing by the corner of the office and be amazed that it is good to be alive. That's what matters in life

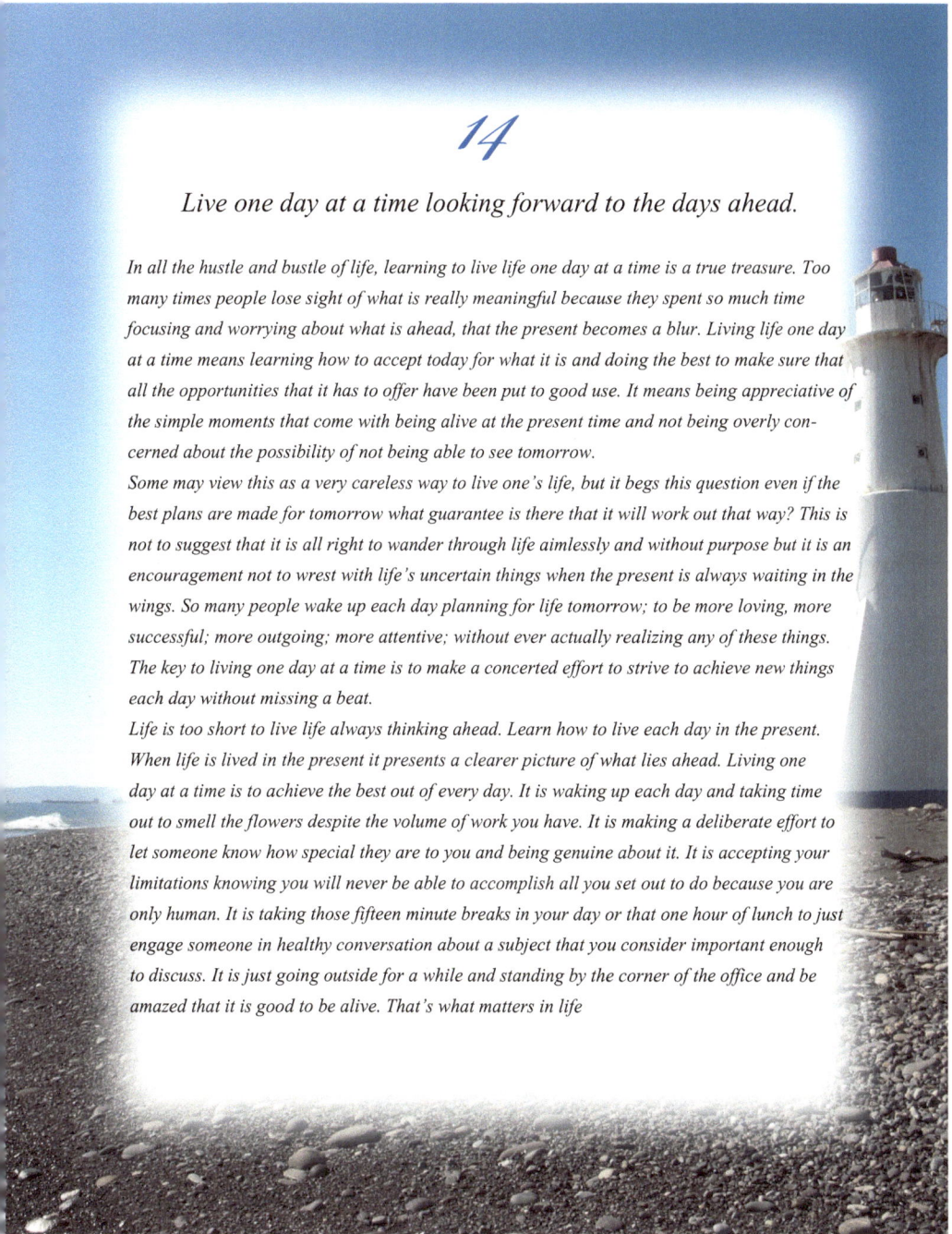

15

Live in the present, honour the past, while preparing for the future.

Being appreciative of the past is often difficult for many people because of what it represents for them. Often times when we look back at where we were it brings back a flood of painful memories. There are those who would rather forget the past, not fully understanding that the past has also helped to shape who they are today. Yes, sometimes the past is best left where it belongs, behind us. But there are other times when the past becomes so important that it is impossible to move forward without embracing it. Dwelling in the past will do little or nothing to help your present circumstances but having a healthy respect for it may be the difference between failure and success. It is difficult to have any kind of meaningful future without reflecting on the past. Where you are now in your life may be as a result of what you did or did not do in the past. Even if our past brings memories of pain and anguish there are lessons that can be learned from having gone through those difficulties. The past often reminds us that we don't have to choose to be victims of our circumstances. We can use those hard lessons to mold us into people who will not buckle under pressure every time the road gets rough.

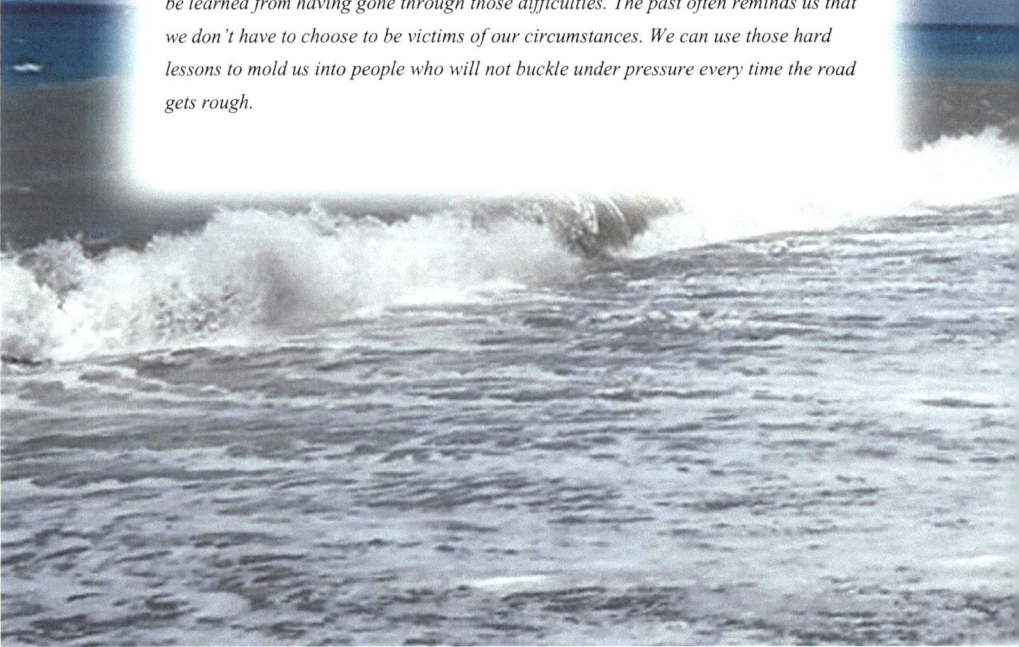

16

As many times as you fall you have the opportunity to rise to success.

The key to falling down is not staying down, it is getting up and moving on with the lessons learned while you were down. When a baby is learning the tedious task of walking, falling down several times a day becomes a part of their routine. But one thing that is always amazing they rarely fall down the same way twice. Each time they get up from falling down it seems they learn the lesson of how not to fall again and so it makes the process of getting up and continuing the process of learning to walk so much easier. In other words, as many times as we fall, the opportunity of getting up to be successful is so much greater because we have a lesson in how not to fall again.

Since falling down is a part of life and you must be prepared for it. Don't worry too much that you will eventually fall down flat on your face for one reason or another. But rather make preparations that when you do fall that you are going to get up again and move towards success. You falling down is not an excuse to give up but rather an opportunity to learn how do what it takes to get you where you really want to go. Don't allow falling down to be the thing that defines you. Don't become known for falling down often, become famous for getting up all the time.

Be like the baby who gets up each time after falling because it just has to figure out how this walking thing works. You just have to figure out how this success thing works but you can't do it lying on the ground of failure. Opportunities that lead to success are most times found focusing on things above or ahead. When you fall don't tell yourself that you are a failure but tell yourself you are a learner who has no plans of staying down. Pick yourself up each time you fall, brush yourself off and seek out the opportunity from your past experience. You may find out that falling down is not so bad after all.

17
Build your foundation with things that last.

A proper foundation is important to anything that is lasting. This is not only true for physical structures, but also to the quality of our lives as human beings. The things we value will determine the kind of life we choose to live and the legacy we leave behind. No sturdy foundation can be built by pursuing things that fade away with time. In the final analysis the foundation we build is greatly determined by the strength of our characters. If our lives are going to be worth living our foundation will have to be one that can stand the test of time.

So what are the things that build a foundation that will last? Honesty and integrity are two good building blocks to begin with. These may sound like clichés but nothing that you and I could ever own in this world can be as valuable as honesty and integrity. They may never make us rich but we are definitely guaranteed a good night's sleep. Building your foundation with honesty and integrity can open many doors of opportunity. When people can trust you for whom you present yourself to be, they have very few problems with giving you the best of themselves.

A keen sense of dependability and responsibility will also make your foundation for life stand firm. These two elements are difficult to find in individuals in today's "dog eat dog" world. It is not always about what you can get out of a task that is the most important thing but rather how you apply yourself to making sure the outcome is your best work. People should be able to trust your word and be confident that you will not disappoint them. Even after the things you have accumulated fade away with time your character will speak volumes about the person you are.

18

The greatest ministry in the Kingdom of God is the ministry of servitude.

This is one of the very personal lessons that I have learned over the years. I used to think that I could find fulfillment in having the right job, a plethora of qualifications and being able to afford all the finer things in life. This is an illusion that people find themselves chasing after most of their lives, only to end up feeling cheated because of the wasted years and unfulfilled dreams. Life is not about what you can get out of it but more about who we have served with our lives. Jesus Christ Himself says that a man's life does not consist in the abundance of earthly possessions (Luke 12: 15). The greatest ministry on earth is to be involved in ministering to people.

A life of service is the trademark of a healthy Christian life. Those who live to serve do so with the understanding that we do this not because of what we can get out of it but for the simple reason that this is what our Lord would have us do. Jesus' life was a true testimony to how a servant should function in a world where it is not the norm to give service onto to others. When we learn how to give service without the frills and thrills we empty ourselves of who we were and become more of what Christ wants us to be.

The Christian who cannot give himself in full service to God is one who does not understand the depth of God's sacrifice in Jesus Christ. Jesus Christ became the ultimate servant (Philippians 2: 5-11) not because He had to, but because this was the only way we mere mortals could comprehend what true service means. He gives us another example when there was misunderstanding among His disciples of what true greatness meant in His kingdom (John 13: 1-17). He took on the role of a lowly slave to provide insight as to what true greatness was. If we desire to be of service to God we have to learn how to live to serve.

19

*Use the negative things people say about you to build a
stronger foundation.*

*It is a very difficult thing to have to listen to others speak negative things about you.
If you live long enough you come to realize that this is one thing that you can do little
to avoid, negative people will always have negative things to say. The difficulty is not
really listening to negative speech but rather to use this negativity as a way of
building a stronger foundation for your eventual success. People will say negative
things but the choice is yours as to what you will do about them. You can choose to
drown in defeat or you can decide to swim along with current towards success.
Don't allow negative speech to destroy the best of who you are but use it as the
cement that holds together your successful foundation. Every time someone say you
can't do something commit yourself to proving them wrong. Each time someone tells
you are not worth it prove them wrong by showing them how valuable you are. Stop
paying so much attention to what the naysayers are saying and use their negative
pronouncements to fulfill your purpose. The greatest occupation of negative people is
to destroy the dreams of others, the greatest tragedy in life is for people with purpose
to lend them a listening ear.*

*Negative people will say negative things; they can't help it. But the choice is always
yours whether or not to listen. If you do choose to listen use it as material to
strengthen your foundation. Negative words can serve as great motivators, for there
is no better feeling than staring into the eyes of someone whose has said negative
things about you and let them know you have not been defeated. Negative words are
like venom from the serpent's mouth, but if taken in the right spirit can be like honey
oozing from the comb. Use the negatives that people have to say about you to help you
build a stronger foundation.*

20

Each challenge faced is one more building block in your house of success.

Approach life's challenges as if you are building a house. After a sturdy foundation has been laid the blocks begin to be added one by one. As the blocks are laid from the foundation up the house gradually begins to take shape. The roof of the house can't go up until the final block has been laid, the different rooms of the house are shaped by these blocks; almost everything about this house is somehow connected to those building blocks. Finding success through challenges will often make you remember building blocks.

Your challenges are simply building blocks that you continue to add to your foundation that has already been laid. Just like the house where the blocks have to come together in order to give it its shape; so it is that your success is shaped by your challenges adding them one block at a time. Each time a difficult circumstance threatens to make you lose sight of your goal, remember it is just one more block that will tell the story of your success. Each time you feel like you are falling apart a block has already been placed in the foundation and it is therefore going to result in a stronger house.

As with real life building blocks if they are just sitting in the yard they are basically useless. All the things you believe you can do and all the things you know you can do are worth absolutely nothing if you don't find the courage to do them. Don't waste your building blocks by failing to grasp the opportunities that come your way to build a sturdy structure of success. Another reality about building blocks is that if they stay too long in the elements they tend to crumble with time. If we fail to use our building blocks they will fast become the ideas that other people will use to build their own lives of success.

21

Tell yourself often that you are worthy of happiness and you will begin to believe it.

Someone wise once said to me that if you tell yourself something often enough you will eventually begin to believe it. Though this is often used when talking about negative things it is also very applicable to positive conversation. The sad truth is that we often don't engage in positive conversations with ourselves and so we live our lives believing we are unworthy of experiencing great things, including happiness. The first stage of being happy is to begin by declaring that happiness is a state you will choose to enjoy in spite of your circumstances.

Positive self-talk is important to our development. What we believe about ourselves and what we deserve affects the way we go about living of lives daily. If we convince ourselves that we are not worthy candidates for experiencing happiness, we will go about seeking only after those things which bring us unhappiness. Happiness has little to do with what we have in our hands but more to do with the state of our mind. Some of the wealthiest people in the world today don't enjoy happiness because they are troubled in their souls.

Begin every day by telling yourself that today I am going to be happy because I deserve it and see how much it alters your perception of life. When we count ourselves worthy of happiness it sets off a chain reaction that begins to affect even the lives of people around you in a positive way. Tell yourself every day that you refuse to allow anything real or perceived to affect what you know to be true. That you deserve to be happy living in this moment. Happiness is not an illusion but rather a purpose driven destination that comes about as a result of what you believe about yourself. Say it often and say it loud, you are worthy of happiness and you just might begin to believe it.

22

The greatest motivation is to prove the naysayers wrong.

As you go through life people will try to determine your future by telling you that it is impossible for you to achieve something things. There is no greater satisfaction than making up your mind to prove them wrong. You cannot sit and live in hope that everybody will believe in your abilities, there are actually more people around who will believe in your failure. If you keep on listening to the naysayers, you will eventually begin to believe and rob yourself of the joy of what could have been.

Rather than allowing the negatives that people have to say make you an underachiever use these negatives as a stepping stones to your success. Every time someone tells you that you can't set out to prove them wrong. Give no one the power to speak over your life, you and God are the masters of your destiny. The only power that people can have over us is the power we are willing to give to them. It is indeed a tragedy when others tell us we are not fit to succeed and we play right into their hands by believing in their negativity. The greatest motivation in life is to stand on the pinnacle of success and smile down at the naysayers.

Motivate yourself to listen to your own voice that keeps screaming that you can be much more than what others are saying. Refuse to give anyone the satisfaction of saying "I told you so", remember that you were created for greatness. The only one that has the power to tell you that you can't is God and you don't have to worry about Him doing that. He created us in His own image and likeness therefore we are creatures of success.

23

Begin each day telling yourself,
"I am destined for greatness".

Today I will tell myself this is my time, it is my day; today I am destined for greatness. Yesterday I may not have believed in me, I may have failed at just about everything I attempted to do, but today I am choosing to believe in my God given abilities. Today I am saying that nobody can stop me, nobody will have the opportunity to put me down because I am destined for greatness. Today I am taking charge, I am taking back who I am from those who see no good thing in me. I am refusing to lay down and play dead because then the naysayers would win. I begin today by shouting it out loud and clear that I am destined for greatness.

Today I will not stand in anyone's shadow, I am going to step out into the light of success and take control of my destiny. Yesterday you told me I was no good and I believed but today I will listen to you no more because I am destined for greatness. You will try to deceive me, you will try to use my negative thoughts against me; you will even go as far as using the people I love to stop believing in me, but I refuse to heed your voice because I know I am destined for greatness. I will not allow your ramblings to overtake my consciousness; I will not pay attention to negative pronunciations or give you room to invade my success because today I am destined for greatness.

I will tell myself this truth every day until I can say it no more. As I wake up to the sound of the morning breeze and see the sun rising above the horizon I will greet the world with calm assurance that today is my day. I will face each challenge that life throws at me knowing that I am standing tall in the eyes of God. It matters not what the world thinks of me, I am fashioned in the image and likeness of a creator who knows no boundaries. I am a child of greatness, so who are you to tell me otherwise. Nobody can stop me because I am on the move towards a higher purpose. I will not allow yesterday's disappointments to determine the path I take today because today I am destined for greatness.

24

When you believe in the value of you being on this earth, you will breathe each moment with pleasure.

It is sad that most times people are credited as being valuable because of some perceived great achievement they have made. So many people will go through life believing that because they have not achieved some significant feat they are less valuable than others who are recognized by society. Being valuable has little to do with achievements, being valuable has much to do with the fact that we are all born this way. By virtue of the fact that we are here means that the possibility of any of us contributing to the world is limitless. When we believe in our own value we will not allow anyone to determine where our place should be and what contributions we should make.

We are not valuable because of a 4.0 GPA; we are not valuable because we were born into the right family; we are not valuable because we have the right complexion; we are not valuable because we can hang around the right crowd; we are valuable for the simple reason that this is how we were meant to be. It is our right to believe that we are powerful beyond measure, not because someone gave us permission to feel this way but because it is a resounding truth. We don't need the approval of any other human being to take to the skies and accomplish great things. All we need to do is to start believing in our own value and tell ourselves we have a purpose.

If we keep telling ourselves every day that we are people of purpose, imagine the worlds that we could conquer. When we believe in our own value welcome each with an assurance that we are more than conquerors. Having value means a refusal to accept mediocrity; it is learning how to see the world and its possibilities through glasses that do not recognize limitations. It is saying to ourselves we can, when everybody around us is telling us that we can't. Our value keeps on appreciating even when circumstances around us depreciate, but it begins with us telling ourselves that we are worth more than gold. Of all God's creatures we are truly the most valuable.

25

Great men and women leave behind a legacy of service after they die

The measurement for greatness can be subjective. Some measure greatness by wealth and achievements, but the greatest measurement for greatness is the legacy that lives on when we leave this earth. We all have the opportunity to walk this earth once in a lifetime and very few people will remember the majority of us. But those who have built a legacy through their actions will continue to live on forever. How will the world remember us when we are gone? What will those who knew us say about us? When people speak our names will it be with affection and sweet reminiscence or fleeting thoughts holding little relevance?

Great men and women do not strive to be remembered by wealth and fame but by the legacy of a life of serving others. The books of history tell memorable stories of men and women who served the world with the radiance found only in the purity of the soul. From legacies of Martin Luther King Jr. to Mary Seacole; we call to memory the legacies of Mahatma Gandhi and Mother Theresa and this list would be incomplete without mentioning own national heroes and heroine. From the stalwarts Norman Washington Manley and Alexander Bustamante to the poor people's Governors Paul Bogle and George William Gordon; the indomitable spirit of Nanny of the Maroons to the visionary Marcus Mosiah Garvey and last but by no means least the uncompromising Samuel Sharpe.

We do not remember these people because they had an abundance of wealth, walked in the right circles, had the most sophisticated education but simply because they lived to serve others. They were not concerned about frills and thrills, status or crowns like so many who live today. They gave their lives willingly in service so that this world that we now enjoy could be a better place for us and our children. Their legacy continues to live through their great acts of compassion and sacrifice. Their names will never be blotted out of the annals of history. Those of us who strive for greatness would do well to remember that great men and women leave behind a legacy of service when they die.

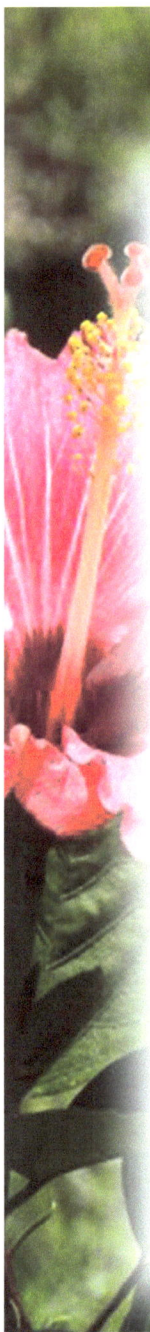

26

Choose to live above the ordinary,
God made you extraordinary.

You are by no means ordinary, you were never created to be ordinary and no matter what you do you can't help being extraordinary. If you settle for being average you will only be satisfied doing just enough to get you by, you will never be curious enough to look behind the door to see what is waiting there. Being extraordinary is to take life by the horns and say to yourself I am going to wrestle with you until you submit because I will never give up. You are by no means ordinary for the simple reason that you were created in the image of an extraordinary God.

Ordinary people do ordinary things, extraordinary people take ordinary situations and turn them into glorious endeavours. Don't be afraid of challenging yourself to find your extraordinary purpose and when you do find it work at it with all you have to give. Think outside the box because true visionaries are extraordinary. No ordinary person has etched their names in the annals of history. Being extraordinary means to yourself conquering the mountain while others are still considering the climb.

Be extraordinary simply because you can't help it, you have found your purpose. You can't be stopped, you are on a mission and you must see it through. You are more than what you see standing before you a gift waiting to be unwrapped. Ordinary people who are often remembered to have been extraordinary are difficult to forget. Let the world remember you for the things that you accomplished despite the doubts of others. Let the world say that it was good to have known you because you did not settle for less. Let the world remember you as a truly extraordinary human being.

27

Nobody will pave your way to a successful life.

Taking charge of your life is probably the most important thing you will ever accomplish. There are few handouts in this world and the probability of you being among the lucky few who gets one of them is very slim. Don't depend on the people around you to do what you ought to be doing for yourself. The road to success is paved with opportunities but you will not have access to them if there is no commitment to taking charge of your life. At the end of the day if you are not successful most of the blame will land squarely at your own feet.

A successful life is not waiting for you in the shadows and it is certainly not lurking around the corner. You are responsible for where you end up in this life, therefore you must take charge of the road that is prepared for you to get there. Think of the satisfaction that you will feel when you have charted your own course? And finally stand on the pinnacles of success through your hard work. It is your life nobody is willing to take responsibility for your ultimate success or failure. Be bold enough to not only dream but to also pursue your dreams with every ounce of strength and determination you can muster.

Too many times people are willing to sit in leisure hoping that someone else will bear the burden of their success. It is not that we don't want to succeed, the problem is that not many persons are willing to do what it takes trod the road of success. You must dare to be different; you must want to be different because you are the master of your own success. Believe that you can complete the journey even through the many adversities you may encounter. It is your life; you have to decide what the best way to live it is. You can choose to be proactive and chart your own course or you can simply succumb to the voice of failure.

28

Give me a mountain to conquer and watch me do it with dignity.

As we look around us we will realize that there are always those people who succeed against the odds. Not only have they conquered their many mountains but they have done so in glorious fashion. Mountains in our lives are not objects of defeat, they are only hurdles in way that we need to create strategies for to over them on our way to success. Yes, these mountains may fall down upon us from time to time but we will never yield to their weigh. Because we are more than conquerors we will always find the strength the get up from among the rubble and keep pressing despite it may cause us.

What would life be without mountains? How can we stand proud in our success if we have not been tried and tested by our mountains falling on us at some point in our lives? The problem often does not rest in the mountain itself but rather from the perspective which we view the mountain. Is your mountain an obstacle to get over or is it a something to buckle under? You may have to go up on the rough side of the mountain but imagine the view that you witness when you finally reach the top. There are many mountains we will have to climb as we go through life. As soon as we have conquered one mountain another will takes its place. The size of the mountain does not really matter it is our decision to conquer that will make the difference. We allow the mountain to come crashing down around us or we can stand in confidence and say give me this mountain knowing that we are more than conquerors. Our mountains serve a purpose, they are there to remind us of how far we have come and yet how we still have to go. Whatever our mountains represent to us be sure to hold on to the assurance that we can climb them step by step and eventually look over into the promise land.

29

I have never seen success give in to failure.

One of the noticeable things about successful people, is that they never stop trying. It's not that they did not have to deal with the pains of failure but for them failure was not an option. Successful people have mastered the art of having a never give up, never give in mentality. For them even when the glass is standing half empty for them it is half full. They are able to use their failures as tools equipping them for success. They live and breathe positive energy, they simply don't give in to failure.

Nobody who sees failure as an ever present obstacle is likely to be successful. We must be ready to accept that failure is indeed a major part of life and for the most part unavoidable. With this in mind we must programme our minds to learn valuable lessons from the things we fail at and use them to bring us a step closer to success. When we give in to failure we truly rob ourselves of the joy of trying again and eventually conquering that mountain we thought was standing between us and a successful life.

To be successful you will have to make a conscious decision not to buckle under the weight of failure. If we give in to failure, we will never know what lies on the other side; sometimes it is necessary for us to fail our way to a successful life. This is not suggesting that we must become comfortable with failing it is simply accepting that if we don't fail we will not learn how to navigate our way through life. The successful people of this world who have failed have great testimonies to share of valuable lessons they learned to pass on to others who are on a similar journey.

30

Success is ninety percent mindset.

Many people don't taste success because they have the wrong mindset. Success is ninety percent mindset because it mostly what you tell yourself that you can that you actually end up doing. If you keep telling yourself that life is an impossible mountain to climb you will no doubt live your life placing various obstacles in your path that you refuse to get over. Change your mindset towards success and watch yourself take each challenge with excitement and expectation.

The mind is a powerful tool that none of us can afford the luxury of wasting. Train your mind to think positive and you will have very little problems seeking ways to be successful. Yes, success can indeed be difficult, but with the correct mindset you will also be convinced that it is not at all impossible. The right mindset will go exploring ways and means to overcome obstacles rather than giving in to defeat. Even if you fail at it once or twice having the right mindset will inform you that it is not over until it is over and it is only over after we have had success.

One key element in having the right mindset towards success is paying close attention to what successful people are doing around you. Successful people don't waste time drowning themselves in the sorrow of defeat, having the correct mindset pushes them to get up, dust themselves off and give it another try. Such people will keep on repeating this activity until they figure out what they have been doing wrong and move on to making sure that they get it right. It is all about having the right mindset.

31

Learn to live like a prospect rather than like a suspect.

The kind of person we strive to become will greatly be determined by the way we choose to live our lives. We can either choose to live above board and keep our integrity intact or we can choose to live a life of suspicion because of our actions and associations. Whatever choice we make will either give those around us the ammunition of viewing us as prospects or suspects.

Living above board can be a difficult mantra to live by, but the dividends paid out can have lasting effects. On the other hand, you may choose to live by suspicious devices and may even get away with it for a time but somewhere along the road it is going to catch up with up. The greatest reward is knowing that that all our accomplishments have come through living a life that can hold up under scrutiny.

Choose to live like a prospect rather than like a suspect. Make it a priority in your life that people can have confidence in your words and actions at all times. Honesty and integrity are hallmarks of success even if the world says otherwise. You may get by cutting corners and make just make a lot of money out of it but the one thing you can never achieve if are true to yourself is the satisfaction and reward of hard work.

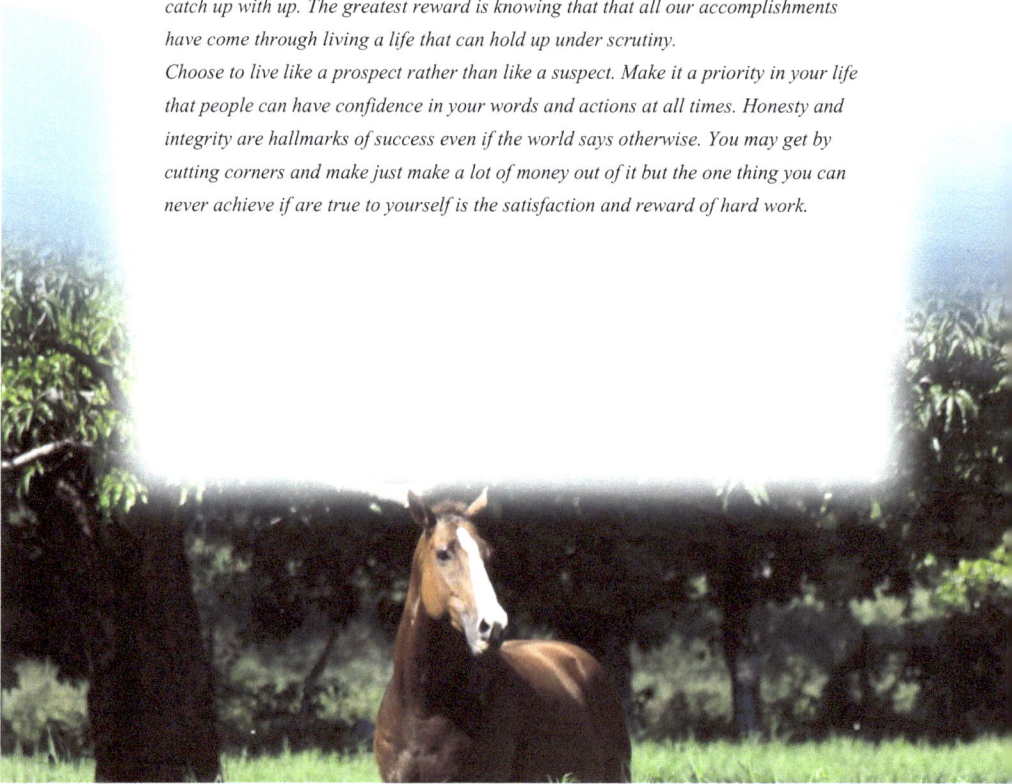

32

The worst thing is to look back at your life only to discover you have not lived.

At the end of it all what will life have to say about you? Have you lived the best life that you could? Or did life just pass you by? This is one thing that scares so many people even if they will not admit it. Imagine spending precious time chasing after things that you thought would have brought you fulfillment only to discover that with all you have gained you forgot to live. It gives great pleasure to be able to look back at your life knowing that you took the time to indulge in the things that are truly meaningful. The worst thing is to look back at your life only to discover you have not lived.

Crowding our lives with unimportant and unrealistic goals will rob many of us of the joy of just simply living. There is absolutely nothing wrong with having goals and expectations, it is something that we should all encourage. But to make them the centre of our world to the point that we forget that life is still going on around us while we chase after them is truly to our detriment. We so often forget what it means to just sit and enjoy a meal because we are forever chasing after something; we no longer stop to have healthy conversations as something may need our immediate attention; the world of beauty passes us by each day because there is somewhere that we just have to get to.

Life is already too complex to live not enjoying the small things. These small things are what make life worth living. Don't settle for hearing other people talk about how much they enjoy living, just wake up and start living. Live each day as if it was your last day on earth, make a deliberate effort to do something you have never done before, you will not regret it. Give yourself a reason to walk along life's garden and begin to smell the roses. You will never realize how much goodness in the world we missed out on because we waste so much time doing what will not matter in the end. Don't risk looking back at your life only to realize that you have never really lived it. Today may be that one chance you get to do something spectacular.

33

Distract negativity from your life by learning how to think positive.

Sometimes in life we need necessary distractions. Too many times we allow our minds to breed negativity by outlook on life. If we cultivate positive thinking and becomes a habit, we will have far less opportunity to heed the voices of negativity. Some wise person once said "as a man thinks so is he" a statement that can be qualified as a truism. Whatever the mind cultivates whether positive or negative it has the power to control our actions and our eventual destiny. Negativity is all around us, it is like a parasite that seeks to choke the life out of anyone it can sink its roots into. The only way to beat the power of negativity is to nullify it by learning how to cultivate positivity in our lives.

Positivity begins with learning how to control our thought process. If we sit each day and invite negativity in our space, it should not surprise us when we begin to live out this reality in our daily activities. Positive thinking is hard work that pays huge dividends, it is easy to harbour negative thoughts and feeling because they not much will be demanded from us. Positive thinking on the other hand will require us to be deliberate and responsible about almost every action we choose to undertake.

Distract negativity from your life by learning how to replace destructive thoughts with positive pictures of success and fulfillment. The mind is a powerful tool that is so often underutilized because what we choose to take into it devalues everything else. We must order our world with things that will get us to our final destination and this begins with a mind that is programmed to think positive. Refuse to accept what the negative voices are saying but listen keenly to that inner voice that is as a constant reminder that we are all people with purpose.

34

There is no greater power than the power of determination.

Determination makes a difference in whether you succeed or fail. It takes grit to overcome obstacles that constantly place themselves in our path. When everything around you says give up it is not worth the effort it is the power of determination that rings out saying keep on pressing on the journey is not yet over. This spirit of determination is what separates men and women from those who only too anxious to make all kinds of excuses as to why they can't succeed. It is that the determined have never failed at anything, but even their failure they committed to raising themselves up to fight another day.

The power of determination gives purpose to the believer. If we have not bought into the idea that we are all here to fulfill a purpose, then we have no reason to be determined. The power of determination will propel us to realizing new heights that we never thought could be reached. It compels us to keep on hoping despite the many things that threaten to thwart our progress. Determinations pays little attention to the voices of pessimism, it gives no quarter to people around us who have never able to put their faith in the pursuit of our purpose. The power of determination will have us rising again and again because our will is stubborn and does not know how to accept defeat.

The power of determination compels us to hold on even when the ship has capsized and the last of the lifeboats have already gone ashore. It's not that we are going to sit and anticipate another lifeboat to come along, but we would instead use all the resources available to make a lifeboat of our own. Determination knows the pain of lost and the tragedy of sorrow; it understands the bitterness of disappointment and the caustic aroma of betrayal. Yet in all of this determination will still say it's not time to pull the cards but rather we must shuffle the deck and play another hand. There is absolute power in the power of determination.

35

The fact that people feel inadequate in your presence does not mean you should not strive to give your best efforts.

It may be difficult to understand but a great number of persons in the world are afraid to strive for success because of how others around then may react. Many refuse to give of their best because others around them may not be comfortable living in their shadow. The discomfort that others have being around successful people may have little to do with the person in question but more about the inadequacy of people who are unwilling to take on life. People who have worked hard to be successful in their lives must not give in to playing victim but should strive to do their best at all times no matter how others feel about our success.

This does not in any way suggest that we should become snobs and flaunt our success in the faces of people around us but we ought never to feel guilty about being successful. No matter how hard you try you will never able to please everybody, which means you will always have people around who feel as if they don't measure up to you whether consciously or unconsciously, it's really no fault of yours. There will be those who will hate us for no logical reason and will work over time to destroy us, but still we must do our best work at all times. People will tell us that we are show-offs, know-it-alls and goody-two-shoes among other things that not even a sinner would repeat on Sunday, but still we must do our best.

Be humble but confident in all your actions only your best is good enough. Feeling small because someone else can't deal with success does nothing to help them, as a matter of fact it does a huge disservice. Allow people around us to see us basking in the light of successful living and be willing to help them to get to where we are. We ought not to be hiding away in the closet or throwing ourselves a pity parties because people can't deal with the best that we have to give we must step out and give our best effort at all times. The truth is we may have only one chance to get it right so we must make it count

36

Take from life the important lessons and ensure they are preserved for the next generation.

Continuity is a sure vehicle towards having a healthy future. Many times the important lessons that are responsible for the success of one generation is not preserved for the incoming one. We all have benefited in some way from some life lesson someone has passed on to us. Somebody took the time to point us in the right direction when we were standing at the crossroad of indecision. Therefore, it is the responsibility of each generation to preserve the lessons that bring the next one to the shores of success. People who fail to learn from the past will forever find themselves driving a vehicle of progress that heads in no particular direction.

Those of us who are privileged to be alive today should seriously examine the lives of our parents and grandparents and learn from them. We often hear them saying that they want better lives for us, sometimes this is just their way of saying that they want us to break the cycle. Truth be told we are in a better position today not to repeat the mistakes of the past because we have at our fingertips much more information than our predecessors. But yet we keeping the cycle of lost hopes and dreams spinning because somehow we never learn. We ought to accept that those before us did not know it all but they survived because they were able to accept and work within the boundary of their limitations.

What story will we ask the generation coming after us to write? We want them to write the greatest one that has ever been written, but it will not happen unless they are equipped with the right tools. It will take courage to accept that those coming after us will accomplish more than we ever will. It will take honesty; we have to be being willing to recognize that we have come short so many times in our quest for success. The lessons that we pass on to our children are not always going to be stories of adventure and accomplishment, sometimes they have to be memories of pain and suffering. These are the great stories that will always stand up to the test of time from generation to generation.

37

Success begins with the desire to succeed and ends with hard work.

Drawing from the book "Think Big" by Dr. Ben Carson the catalyst for a successful life begins with the desire to succeed. This means never accepting the reality that others try to paint for you and moving to the beat of your own drum. Our desire for success must be stronger than all the obstacles that will come our way; our desire for success must be the force that drives us towards achieving our goals when all the odds are stacked against us. We will never know how much we can succeed until we are willing to put our abilities to the test and we will never put our abilities to the test until we have a strong desire to succeed.

Along with this desire to succeed goes all the important ingredient of hard work. Very few people in this world have been successful by sitting around and counting cards. Hard work demands forming a consistent habit of seeing things through to the end. So many people in this world have a genuine desire to succeed but so very few have the strength to see things through to the end. Hard work is the end result of the desire to succeed but it is in the process of hard work that we tend to learn some of the most valuable lessons that life have to offer. Hard work takes grit and an attitude of non-acceptance of things that are mediocre. It involves a stubborn refusal to see failure as an option but always looking for the next step up the ladder of success.

Never be satisfied with just simply having a desire for something better, be willing to step out of your comfort zone and go for something better. It's not about how many times we failed but rather how many opportunities we have given ourselves to get it right. It's never how long we take to get there but that we get there no matter how many mountains were standing in our way. It is the unquenchable desire to succeed that will keep us going on and on through the rough and difficult times. When we have nurtured this desire to succeed the only thing that can happen to us is that we come out on the other side of success shining like a coin in mint condition.

38

No one will take interest in you if you choose to be uninteresting.

Each of us have something that is unique about us. This one thing that defines us is what makes us interesting. We often have the false notion that because we are not bright enough, beautiful enough; the correct height or right complexion; brilliant enough or have the right connections that we are uninteresting. We use these things to help us avoid the world looking at us for who we really are, interesting people. The truth is being interesting is not determined by how others perceive us but rather by how we perceive ourselves, we are interesting not because we fit some standard or criteria, but simply because we were born interesting people.

We can choose to be uninteresting and pine away at our ordinary lives or we can choose to live interesting by discovering our purpose. Nothing about us is ordinary, just about anyone of us has within us what it takes to turn this world upside down. We have with us the capability of

doing even greater things than the people we so often idolize. Have ever given thought to the fact that many of these people at some point may have been told or even believe they were uninteresting people. The only difference between such persons and us is that they refuse to believe or accept what others had to say about them. We often resign to be uninteresting people because we become too caught up in what others have to say about our abilities. No one will take interest in us if we choose to constantly fly under the radar of being ordinary. We must give ourselves a chance and be open to discovering what is it about us that everybody else would want to know. We must present ourselves as a package waiting to be unwrapped, revealing the world's greatest treasure, an interesting person. This person who will go above and beyond to what the world says to make a mark in this great universe or rewrite the pages of history. Interesting people will always do interesting things, we do this world no justice by

settling for an uninteresting existence

39

Give yourself a chance to live above your circumstances.

A number of people in this world have been able to overcome extreme difficulty to live successful lives. One of the key things that is always noticeable with such persons is their resilience. They did not allow their circumstances to define them but chose to live above them. The power to do this lies in every person it is just a matter of how you look at life. Are you a glass half empty or a half glass full type of individual? Where we end up in our lives will be significantly depend on how we view the circumstances that we must face one way or another. Do we use our circumstances to motivate us to do great things or do we drown ourselves in the falsehood of not being born with the opportunities that others have had? It is indeed true that some people are presented with more opportunities but even the best of us have failed miserably at any task if our attitude is wrong, no matter how many opportunities we have at our disposal.

Live above your circumstances by having a glass always half full mindset. You will never be able to control many of the circumstances in your life, but you can certainly choose how they shape you. Too many people are comfortable living in their circumstances rather than working at coming out of their circumstances. Nothing is owed to us, the most successful people in this world are people who saw what they wanted to achieve and went after it diligence and purpose. If one individual is able to achieve success by overcoming their circumstances, then it is a sure thing that all persons have the same power lying with them. Change the way how you thing and it is almost a guarantee that you will begin to unlock your potential.

Give yourself a chance to live above your circumstances because if you don't the only person that you will be hurting is you. One of the tragedies of life is the vast amount of people in this world that have fulfilled their purpose. Don't be counted among these persons because you had the wrong outlook on life. You may not be where you want to be at this time; it may take you a very long time to get there; you may even have many failures and heartaches along the way, but if you are truly committed to getting there image the joy that emanate from your soul when you finally do. Your circumstances don't define you, circumstances are merely temporary hurdles that we need to get over in order to get to our destination and that destination is success and greatness.

The longer I live the more I realize I will walk this road only once.

I will walk this road only once so while I am doing this I will do the best that I can. No matter how many plans I make to do change the world I am very much aware that the opportunity to do so may be once in a lifetime. I am therefore committing to live each day of my life deliberately looking out for that opportunity. I am not going to be satisfied with just simply playing with the idea of receiving my "big break" because the fact is that "big break" has been before me all the time. I do not plan to change the world tomorrow because I live in the reality of what happens today. Today is always the best day to do something exceptional, if tomorrow arrives then it presents an equal opportunity to add to my achievements of yesterday.

Life is definitely too short to settle for looking back with regrets at the things I did not allow myself to do. I know too many people who are now looking back at their most productive years being bitter because they failed to reach for the stars when they had the opportunity. I may have the chance to do several things in one lifetime, but that one thing that sets me apart from the rest of ordinary people takes guts and grit. I don't want to be remembered because of fame and fortune, I want to be remembered because I did not resign myself to an ordinary life, but I took a chance to walk the road less travelled.

I will walk this road only once so here is what I am going to do. I am going to embrace each day as if it were my last day on earth. I will seek to make a meaningful impact on the life of even one individual every day. I will step outside of my comfort zone and give my-self to a worthy cause, something worth dying for. I will laugh more often, I will smile at the world even when there is little to smile about, the world indeed need more people who smile. I will be grateful whether I have an abundance or I find myself in dire distress. I will make a sacrifice for the good of somebody who needs it. I will take nothing for granted because I will walk this road only once and will walk as one who has discovered the joy of living a full life.

Listen to that voice that keeps telling you, you can become more than you are now.

The voice of doubt is a curse to the human spirit. If you continue to tell yourself that you are going nowhere in your life don't be surprised if you eventually get nowhere. The voice of doubt is like a lying spirit meant to keep us subdued until it has destroyed the very core of our being. The sad truth is that we often pay much attention to that voice of doubt than we do to that voice that continually tells us that we can become much more than we are now. That voice that keeps ringing in our ears that tell us we were placed here on this bountiful earth to accomplish great things. This is the inner voice of truth that will always speak in ways that draw out the best that is in us if we just stop and listen but for a little while.

Our inner voice of truth is the voice that we should give our undivided attention. That voice that keeps telling us that we are without limits, that voice which tells us to step out and take a chance at doing something bold and different. The inner voice of truth reminds us that though things may not be at the very best for us now but if we stick to the script eventually we will reap the fruits of our labour. It keeps us grounded in the darkest of times and restores our hope when our mountains come crashing down around us. Our inner voice of truth helps us to focus on the fact that we are not failures, it is just that it is taking us a longer time to get to where we need to be. Listen to your inner voice of truth and stop swimming in the sea of self-doubt and unfulfilled dreams. Whatever your inner voice of truth tells you to do step put in faith and go and conquer. You are much important to this world than you will ever understand, without it life would never be the same. Listen keenly to that voice that keeps telling you to be the best that you can be even the circumstances of your life just don't seem to add up. Your inner voice of truth is who you really are and if you just give it a chance you will learn how to see the world through a different pair of eyes, the eyes of truth.

42

Surround yourself with people who will get you where you want to go.

The road to success is very difficult for the average person. This difficulty is significantly multiplied if you surround yourself with the wrong persons. Many of the people we interact with on a daily basis will add very little to our lives, but these are the very people we also often think we can't do without. Whether or not we are willing to admit it, many of the persons we associate with are stumbling blocks to us being successful. If you have any dream of being a world changer you will have to pay keen attention to the people you invite into your space.

My grandmother told me once that "the train to nowhere is overloaded with willing passengers". I am only now beginning to appreciate the wisdom of these words if you spend your time being around people who are going nowhere you should not too surprised when you do get to nowhere. Surround yourself with people who share your dreams and visions, people who will help find your place in this world. What good is it to any of us is being a part of the crowd adds little or no value to us fulfilling our purpose. And sometimes the selfishness of the people we have around us even make them willing to seek success at our expense.

Your inner circle should comprise of people who are helping you work towards your cause while you are doing the same for them. They should never be people who are taking much more than what they give. They should not be people whose only mission is to silently destroy everything good about you while elevating themselves. Surround yourself with people who willing to stand up with you and even die for you if necessary. The people you choose to have around you will make the difference in whether you fail miserably at your goals or up the ladder of success to fulfill your purpose.

43

Upgrade your friends as often as you need to.

We spend a lot of time upgrading our gadgets. As soon as a new phone, tablet, computer or any other gadget comes we want the latest version. We do this because we are aware that the latest model may have features that the previous version did not have that we may find useful or even important to what we want to achieve. Have we ever given the same thought to some of the friends we keep? This is not a suggestion that we must simply discard our friends because they no longer serve our purpose but to seriously examine if whether or not the people that we allow in our space are adding value to our lives. If the people in our lives are taking us away from our main aspirations, if they are failing to motivate us to be go-getters then we may just need an upgrade of our friends.

There are some people in our lives that will have a permanent place. These persons will know the real us. They will stick by us no matter the circumstances, they speak honesty and truth regardless of how much we wear our feelings on our sleeve. They will celebrate your triumphs and weep with you in times of failure. They tell us what they think of your stupid decisions and will also closely monitor us to make sure we make better choices. These are the people we always want to have around us. People who will expose our flaws but offer us a shelter in times of storm. If the people we have in our lives currently don't fit this bill, then we may just need to upgrade our friends.

Friendship is a treasure that should be guarded like a mighty fortress. Those who dare enter within its realms enter into a sacred space, it is therefore important who we choose to allow the privilege of entering. It is better to have few friends you can call your true friends than to have a host of acquaintances that add little value to your mission on earth. The bond of true friendship holds strong even through the most difficult crisis because true friendship is like gold that has been forged by fire to reveal its purity. If those who you call friends would not be willing to stand with you in the heat of battle, then you may just be in need of a friend upgrade.

44

As you walk through life leave your footprints in the sands of time.

Never strive to be someone who is worth forgetting, you are here to make a mark on this wonderful planet. As you walk through life make sure that you leave your footprints on the sands of time. When you have left this earth and people stop to reflect on who you were and what you meant to them let it be with a sense of pride and love that is was indeed good to have known you. It was good to have had the opportunity to engage you into honest and purposeful conversation; it was a joy to have been given the privilege to be graced with your presence; it was great to have shared your friendship through some of the most challenging times. As you go through life do all that is in your power to make the life that you have lived is worth remembering.

You are a priceless jewel in the crown of life, there is no treasure that can be compared to the beautiful soul that is you. As you walk through this life paint with world with the bold colours of your personality, you're a spark waiting to be ignited into a raging fire of goodness and love. People will want to know where your feet have trod in this amazing phenomenon that we call life. They will want to know who you were and what was it that motivated you to walk the way you did on the sands of time. Take nothing for granted there will never be another like you even if we live a million times over, your footprints can never be duplicated.

You have beautiful feet; feet that walk for change and stand up for justice, feet that walk miles at a time to right even a single wrong; feet that find no comfort in the suppression of truth. Your feet will forever alter the landscape of this earth because your footprints are recorded on the sands of time. No matter how rugged this path becomes the sands of time will always preserve your story because it is a story worth telling. There is nothing ordinary about your footprints. Even after your feet have been worn out with usage over time your footprints etched in the sands of time will remain for all to see and to know that you once walked this very same path.

45

*While you journey through life pay close attention to the
signs pointing in the right direction.*

As life takes us from place to place sometimes we don't pay attention to where the
signs are pointing us to go. For every direction we may take there is a sign there that
we need to pay attention to. These signs will help us to avoid many of the mistakes
and pitfalls that will cause us defeat. It is only a fool that will keep going in the wrong
direction upon reading a sign that says detour. But the sad truth is that many of us
take this very approach to how we live our lives. The signs will tell us what direction
we need to go in and we stubbornly ignore them and go in the opposite direction only
to find our lives in turmoil. Pay attention to where the signs in your life are leading
you.

Signs are an important part of who we are and what we eventually become. Sometimes signs tells us to stop or to slow down because we are need of a new perspective
on life. At other times they tell to be full of caution danger there is something ahead
of us that we need to be aware of. Sometimes our signs say caution as a means of
preparing us for the uncertainty of events in our lives. They may even say slippery
slope as a warning to us that the journey towards our goals may be a difficult one and
at other times they will simply say that you have arrived at your destination. Whatever
your signs are saying to you make sure that you take the time to pay close attention.
Each sign will leave a lasting impression on the story of your life. Embrace your
signs, don't ignore what they are trying to say to you or where they leading you. Keep
your signs close to you, they have been placed in your life for a reason. Even when
your signs become obsolete it is a perfect opportunity for new signs to take the place
of the old ones and begin to teach new lessons. Your signs will not always be the same
they will change to bring relevance to your life. If you end up going in the wrong
direction, just stop and look around you and see if you were paying the attention that
you should have to the signs on the road, which is your life.

46

*Make every day the day you do your best work; it may be
your last opportunity to have your name etched in the
pages of history.*

If you had only one chance to make a lasting impression on some task, would it be your best work? What if you were given the opportunity to put down your name on the pages of history, would you do your greatest work possible? Every day that you work at any task give it your all because it may just be the one task that will make your name known throughout the world. Don't be so caught up in looking forward to your big break, give your all to the task at hand. Can you imagine how disappointed you would feel if you were asked what did you do yesterday that is worth remembering? Only to realize that you did not see the opportunity that was right in front of you to make an impact on the world.

History was not written by those who set out to write it but rather by very ordinary people who just went about doing what they were called to do with passion and purpose. It was written by those who diligently stuck to the task or mission given to them even without knowing or understanding the possible outcome. These are the same people if they were alive today would look back at their achievements and ask what did I do to deserve such recognition? I was only doing what I was called to do, I was only fulfilling what came to me so naturally. The thing is that such people had an understanding that they probably would never get an opportunity to do anything of that nature again so they did it with precision once and for all time.

Make each day the day you pull out all the stops to produce your best work. Whatever you are called to do, do it with perfection and pride. If someone should come across what you have done centuries after you have gone they will know that you were once a part of this amazing universe. If you are not going to work hard at any task to produce your best, then what good would it have done you to even make an attempt to begin with? Even if you never receive fame or fortune for your work, a sense of satisfaction and pride will flood your soul just to know that you have held nothing back. Every day that you wake up as you take on the world say to yourself today is the day I will make a difference and do the best work possible.

47

Be prepared for change not once, but several times in your lifetime.

The only thing in life that remains constant is change. Change will take place whether or not we are prepared for it. Dealing with change may be the most difficult circumstance that many people will have to deal with their lives, but it does not have to be an uphill task if we have the right mindset.

The best way to deal with change is to accept the reality that it will happen, no matter what attempts are made to avoid it. If we learn how to live with this fact, we may just find that we will be better able to navigate life's road on the journey to successful living.

Life does not occur in a vacuum. Some may want it to be that way but it would be nothing short of living in a fool's paradise.

Because we already know that change is going to take place, it is a given that there will be some things that we will not be able to control.

Take for example the fact that:

• *We can eat healthy and exercise daily (this is always encouraged) but at some point we will have to accept that we are going to die – this is change.*

• *We can invest in all the best financial instruments but because of circumstances and bad business decisions we may find ourselves broke – this is change.*

• *We can invest in a great product to slow down the aging process but one day it will simply catch up with us – this is change.*

• *We may get the opportunity to work with the best company in the world or pursue the ideal career path but one day the human resources department may remind us that our retirement party is just around the corner – this is change.*

• *The children we convinced ourselves would always be at home and need us will one day tell us that they think it is time to move out – this is change.*

• *As much as we love our spouses it is likely that either we will have to leave them behind or they will leave us to walk the land beyond – this is change.*

So when it comes down to the crux of the matter the only thing that we can afford to do with change is learn how to live with it.

Don't waste valuable time being apprehensive about change, embrace it. We may just find that we enjoy much more of our lives and make time to explore those things that are truly meaningful.

Change is neither a good master nor a bad servant it is simply how we view it that makes the difference. We can choose to swim downstream and allow the currents of change to bring us comfortably to our final destination or we can choose to drown by trying to go against the current. Whatever we decide to do, change will still happen!

Paul A. Blake is a man for all seasons, he is a dynamic presenter with several years of experience in public speaking locally and overseas. He is passionate about helping people to realize their full potential and believes that each individual has within him/herself the tools to unlocking their passions.

He is a graduate of the University of the West Indies, Mona Campus, Jamaica, with a degree in Theology and is in the final stages of a master's degree in Counselling and Pastoral Psychology from the International University of the Caribbean in Jamaica. He is CEO of the company Words Worthit Motivational Speaking and Training Co. Ltd. He is a trained minister of religion and Licensed Marriage Officer. He lectures with the National Youth Service in several areas including personal development, career development and gives motivational presentations and is heavily involved in the Churches of Christ throughout Jamaica and the Caribbean especially in the area of youth development.

Paul has been married to the beautiful and affable Racquel Wynter Blake for eight years and together they have an extraordinary son Timothy-Jordan. His greatest desire is to have all people experience the abundant life that Jesus Christ promise in John 10: 10 "I have come that you might life and have it more abundantly".

www.ingramcontent.com/pod-product-compliance
Lightning Source LLC
LaVergne TN
LVHW010028070426
835513LV00001B/18